YOUR DAILY GUIDE TO SHINE

YOUR DAILY GUIDE TO SHINE

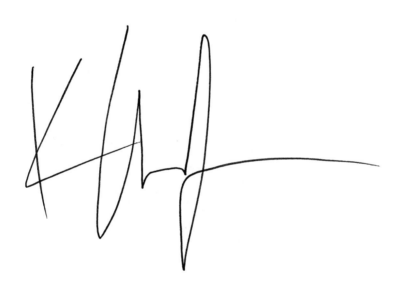

KEVIN ALAN LAMB

Your Daily Guide to Shine

Copyright © 2023 Kevin Alan Lamb

For my Mamyte, and Papa Bear
My brothers, my sisters
My family, my friends
Musicians
Badger
Dixon
And Nancy

Hello, I've been expecting you. You are loved more than you could ever know. You didn't think anyone was listening, but we are. You didn't think anyone noticed, but we did. You didn't think anyone cared, but we do. Thank you for holding onto hope, especially when it's the hardest. You won't always have to carry it alone. We're finding a way to be there for you. We're making time to acknowledge how much we need and appreciate you. I'm sorry our timeline isn't in tune with your own; but how can I help you if I can't help myself? I want you to know that I'm working on me so I can better help you. I'm not the best version of myself every day, but that doesn't mean I don't care, or that I've lost sight of where I hope to grow. I understand that you're likely more similar, than different, to my relationship with myself. I also understand that there's so much I don't understand, including you. But I am here trying, helping, breathing, and being something that might make your day a little better than if I didn't exist.

CONTENTS

CHAPTER 1

ORIGIN STORY

Can you elaborate on the notion of music as providence?

Music goes beyond our understanding. It gives a window to another world. Depending on a person's faith, if they have it, you have to keep a temporary state of everything. There's going to be change, though it feels like it's never going to end. Living faithfully day-to-day, music can be the love people hang onto, even if it's for a couple of hours at a time. When I was in the ER, I'd look at the clock and tell myself, "If she can make it two hours, she will make it."

—Bob Crawford, The Avett Brothers

Some months after interviewing Bob Crawford, adopted brother and bass player of The Avett Brothers, I found myself sitting in a coffee shop just footsteps away from where a burned CD playing on an old stereo, changed my life. You may not be familiar with the American folk-rock band from Concord, NC., but they are my favorite band; and three years after their music inspired me to dream again, I found myself interviewing one of my heroes. From their sixth album, *I and Love and You* (2009) came the song "Head Full of Doubt/Road Full of Promise," and the lyrics which served as the foundation for my greatest adventure. I spent the first 18 years of my life believing that I would pitch a baseball for a living, but fate intertwined when I tore my rotator cuff, and insisted on the opportunity of utilizing my gifts to pursue a dream I hadn't yet considered.

No matter the gifts we are given, it is the ability to feel, focus, align, and commit which wakes our dreams into realities. The words of others helped me find words of my own; but most of all — they gave me permission to believe in big dreams — made possible with their pursuit. No matter the distances I travel, shows that I work, and bands who I fall in love with, it is the words of the humblest, most grateful students of music which help carry, and guide me home. Their lyrics are tattooed on my left and right wrist to hold myself accountable, and always remind me to honor my greatest gift (writing), and ability to positively influence others.

"Decide what to be, and go be it."

—The Avett Brothers

If you are lucky enough the music you love flows through your veins long enough to recreate a world you see, touch, taste, love, and lose in. When something is within you long enough it becomes you. The very way the soul of a man shapes his dreams, music breathes belief into these shapes, sights and sounds, until one day when there is no telling where it begins, and you end. And while it is literally medicine to navigate the weight created by water taken on in the struggle between high and low tide, I am most grateful for the cathedral of awe and wonder from which music has built my love into my life.

"Where you invest your love, you invest your life."

—Marcus Mumford

It is my intention for these words to help you find words of your own, written in the pages that fill your life's story with your passion, purpose, and activities which bring you the greatest joy. Your joy is your light; walk in its direction to discover your true calling and help others to do the same. Music is the vehicle that built my love into my life, what is yours? For nearly a decade I have worked in live music — building community, interviewing bands, photographing events, managing artists, booking and promoting shows — whilst spreading a positive message of love, inclusivity, and joy. What is your guiding light? Which direction is it calling you in? Are you listening? Isn't it time?

CHAPTER 2

HOME

If numbness has replaced the sensation once in your heart, then perhaps it is best you take a moment and gather both the physical and emotional coordinates of where you are. Are you restless where you once found peace of mind? Is the light being drained from your soul a product of the people, places, and activities which occupy your time? Are you lifted, or is it you that always does the lifting?

Lifetimes are spent evaluating progress, performance, and paths we have chosen, yet so little time understanding ourselves, our passion, and our potential. Our greatest weakness is the inability to understand ourselves, our gifts, and the very reasons for which we were given life. Purpose is not always derived from the means by which we pay bills, however, life is given greater enthusiasm when said means is a derivative of our purpose. Most people fear that they cannot do what they love for a living, but that doesn't mean you can't do what you love! We are connected to the stars, but activation occurs only when we open our hearts and minds to the external guidance which perpetually passes in, and out of our sight, touch, and taste.

Inspiration is the trail of breadcrumbs left by Hansel and Gretel for us to find our way home. Edward Sharpe and the Magnetic Zeros, O.A.R., Jack Johnson, The Head and The Heart, Elephant Revival, Billy Strings, and countless other brilliant musicians refer to home in a manner that suggests it is not confined within any specific space or time, rather it exists in all places, in all times, if we are able to maintain our connection with it. With the people, places, and notions such as happiness, care, hope, joy, and love, that we find purpose in.

For that reason — home is a derivative of purpose — discovered within ideas, people, animals, songs, works of art, missions, and causes that activate them. Though long, elusive, and often lacking illumination, a ladder to the stars is imprinted upon their being; upon the very way they breathe, think, and feel. Once activated, the longing for not greatness but purpose, and home in all things, never fades. For some it is a burden; but it is only a burden once we stop listening to the song that sings in our heart. The song that sings our story to the world not to be heard, but to be harmonized, covered, and truly felt on an innate level that reminds others of their home, and their purpose in all things.

Your love simultaneously takes you away from your blood family, but to a whole-nother family. Can you talk about how that's both difficult and satisfying?

Yeah, it's definitely a sacrifice when you leave your family and leave your wife, or your girlfriend, or boyfriend, or whoever you have at home, waiting for you, and you're on the road, thousands of miles away, typically…

Rivers and roads away.

Yeah, that's kind of what that song ["Rivers and Roads"] is – why it still resonates so heavily with us – and I think it encapsulates how we feel on the road. Even though at that time we weren't touring, we were moving across the country, onto different things. But that song is the summary of what this modern life is to everyone I think. Where you strike out on your own, and you have people you come back to – hopefully.

—Tyler Williams, The Head and the Heart

Home exists in those that give you hope. In those that the very thought of brings tears of joy. In those that have seen your goodness shine and will always remind you of it when you need it most. It is in those that will never let you pick up the pieces alone. In those that care more about seeing the smile on your face than anything you could ever give them in return. Home are the shivers inspired by the excitement of reciting lyrics you love from the musicians that sacrificed, and offered you the opportunity to bathe in their creation, while in the company of those that lift your head and your heart when they weigh heaviest. Home is an illusion until you discover the souls that sing in a tune that your very own is drawn to, moved by, and made better in the company of.

(shivers)

No matter the lives we live, the best any of us can hope for is a highlight reel of moments that remind us that we are alive and invested in the pursuit of love, the wild, and wonder. My advice to you in these moments is to cherish them. Take several deep breaths and open your eyes wide to see, and feel, and be infected by the phenomena which you will do your best to understand, appreciate, and internalize, yet somehow inevitably let slip away with exposure to struggle, scrutiny, and the constant bitch of time. The wise man strives to be in harmony with the people, places, sights, and sounds of the universe. The fool attempts to dictate the flow of the universe for his or her personal benefit. Once submerged in the thick of our passion, when our love is invested in our life, we discover home in the people that help us always feel that way. In those who value us for the wild and romantic longings that are realized where chance, will, and spontaneity collide.

(collide)

For some of us the very notion of home is intertwined with a calling to the road. Adventures at the precipice of a dream, and those who usher in its becoming. Passion is interstellar currency, burning at a temperature so palpable that it is sought after, commodified, and planted like seeds gifting others permission to wake their dreams. Lifetimes are spent without taking chances on ideas nor dreams. As a result, there is a natural attraction or magnetism towards those who pursue theirs, and gravitate towards a calling as a career. We are impressionable beings moved by the serendipitous unfolding of another's story. Whether you are a romantic or not, hard work is at the heart of "the occurrence and development of events by chance in a happy or beneficial way."

(serendipity)

In the midst of playing 175 shows in 2016, what are some routines you practice to stay balanced, focused, and grateful?

I think remembering that just because you are the party doesn't mean you have to party every night. This year we were all more focused on our health than we ever were, and it was amazing the difference and impact that had. We strap on our gym clothes every morning and hunt down the most gnarly looking YMCAs all over the country. Even if it's only 45 min, a quick run, a game of PIG on the basketball court and a 10-minute sauna will literally change your life. We try to find time to practice before the show daily, too. Hanging out with fans and doing some signing after the shows really have been important as well and keep us humble and incredibly grateful.

—Andy Dunnigan, The Lil Smokies

I am six days into the longest stretch of sleeping in my own bed since I cannot recall. Six days into seeing the sunset on the water, waking without uncertainty of my whereabouts or what logistics I had to consider for the day's travel ahead. I enjoyed my first boat ride since moving in June, met neighbors, and indulged in the delight of fireside conversation with new friends.

What is a blessing without our willingness or ability to recognize it? Where does joy go when we are not in a place to receive it? Why do we fool ourselves into believing that we will better honor our gifts in a future time, if we do not nurture them today? It doesn't need to happen all at once, but it does need to happen, and taking care of yourself is the best place to begin. I love to travel: I am drawn to the connectivity, natural wonder, and potential of the road, but home is an oasis where I best tend to my garden, honor my energy, and align myself to realize the dreams in my heart.

(oasis)

Truck drivers, tourists, travelers, and musicians surf the highway's paved waves. Some for work, some for play, for others — the lines between are blurred evermore — every day. Beating hearts pound pavement, while the rubber below does the work; there is a ladder to your stars but to find it you must search. Which roads call you home? Have you made your heart's intentions known? Have you taken the time to realize just how much you've grown? We sleep each night, resting for the days to come where our dreams are in sight. These dreams change as we age; take inventory of what you want when setting your aim. Be wary of the pursuit of a vision you no longer see; be mindful of those who expend energy to condemn, criticize, and limit your potential because they do not believe. We are the realization of one another's greatest mysteries, awe, and wonder. Satisfied souls seek not to reduce your magic, standing in the way of another's gifts is tragic. We surf these paved ways to unravel the institution's illusions. Our beating hearts pound pavement to remind us that our tribe grows wide, running as deep as the ocean's depth, moved by her tides, captivated by her breath.

(paved waves)

At 33 I discovered Amtrak trains, forgetting the freeways and exits that all look the same. Seeing the country the way it once was, ride the train and dare fall in love. When did we lose romance, and forget to slow dance, when taking a chance, on our way to falling in love? From Northeast to Midwest I travel, while life's mysteries unravel, no longer a confused poet left to babble. My words are the seeds I need to plant, or my heart will bleed without the chance, for true love and her hand in dance. As we glide through the night, to the tune of delight, under magnificent stars so bright. May we manifest memories, from what were just dreams? Let us travel many miles, with but a few leaps. Does our love become blood, as it seeps to the earth, to feed its beating heart? Might my true love be somewhere out there, riding in an Amtrak car? Might she be reading these very words? Riding these very rails? Or is she in the great wilderness hiking along rivers and trails?

I travel by day, and through the night; the ink of my pen is red with love, I see only distant lights. These pages turn, as the train engine burns, finding its way, but never home. Given purpose in motion, indivisible like an endless ocean. This train is bound for glory, the way I long for true love in my story. We can't quite know where it will go, or which parts comprise the beginning, middle, or end. At sunrise or sunset? Should we flip a coin or bet? At which next turn might I expect, to once and for all lose my breath? Letting go my fear of regret; imagine traveling the world by train, after we have finally met.

(amtrak trains)

On the open road, in backyards, allies, and street corners, I am connecting myself with a disconnected American People. Planting little seeds of hope that with the oddest combination of chance, will, and necessity, will grow into a powerful people, and friend of the desperate. Increasingly connected to the road, each time I travel it, we are fortunate to be blessed with fresh greens and a shining sun, shimmering through the tall trees. We roll closer to our destination where happy, creative people reside, and the music they love. Musicians are among the oldest healers on this planet, born with the passion and need to harness their talents, and share their songs to experience balance. A constant flow of energy pushes and pulls us throughout this journey we travel, positioning ourselves within shouting distance of those called to the resistance of a way that never served our people, nor planet.

(planting seeds)

Heightened focus and clarity, this abundant world with such disparity. Bridging the gap between love and the unknown. Freedom from this faulty foundation, from which we've grown. A house is said to be a home, but can it be without a heart? Difficult to believe we've come this far, with so little progress. Being human is given; being love is learned through compassionate living. On this Tuesday in November I say a prayer to the full moon. Asking to help us rise. Help us heal from our burdens and soften our hate. Help us acknowledge personal struggles, so we may recognize them in another. Help us understand that we are a *human family*: Mothers, fathers, sisters, and brothers. Only love is powerful enough to ask that you heal. Only love will replace the space fear filled in your heart with hope. Only love will unburden the great-weight you carry in tow. Isn't it time to let go? Isn't it time to be free? Isn't it time to believe that we're capable of being better? As you gaze at the moon in the coming days, I ask that you rise. Rise for yourself, so you may rise for others. Rise to shine, and remind yourself that you can. Rise for the earth, to protect these precious and vulnerable lands. Rise for our *human family*, we could use your helping hands.

(a prayer to the full moon)

Can you describe a particularly difficult time in your life where words failed, and music spoke?

Yeah... Oh, yeah. I think we all have lots of those. I think a particularly potent time would be... my brother had died in a room in our house when I was 10, and my sisters and I were living there and my dad kind of transformed the energy of that room. He went to a pawn shop and got a lot of instruments, basically, and filled the room with instruments, and it hadn't been something we could really talk about, it was a pretty traumatic chain of events, so instead, that was kind of our way of communicating. We started off all on drum sets, playing drums, then we slowly brought in a guitar, then an amp and a guitar, then a bass, so we started making music together to communicate through things. We had a brokedown Greyhound bus in our front yard that a band, our oldest sister was a drummer, and her boyfriend at the time became kind of our mentor, and that's how we all started playing music together pretty much - was to get through that.

That's beautiful. Do you feel like you're connected to your brother every time you play?

I do. I feel like it's been… anybody really, no matter what age that's passed on becoming your ancestor, even if they were younger than you when they died. It's an interesting thing, and music connects you with everybody that's been before, it's part of what we don't recognize, exactly what the patterns are, or why they make sense but I think that they are some kind of representation of things that have been, that we still resonate with.

—Bonnie Paine, Elephant Revival

Most of us aren't yet where we hope to one day be, and that's good news. Everyday we wake up with the potential to grow, and be better than we were the day before. Like the ocean's tides we rise and we fall, making space to stumble so we can better learn to chart a steady course in our coming days. More than a million moments, choices, intentions, and actions have brought each of us to this present moment; please consider this before criticizing or condemning yourself, or another because one wasn't the best. We all struggle more than we care to admit, yet these struggles are not what define us; rather our ability and tenacity to use them as fuel to ascend new heights. If life was made of mountaintops, we would not know the sweet nectar of the journey between.

With unlimited growth potential, it is imperative to recognize the limits others bestow upon you (unintentionally, or intentionally). Similarly, take inventory of limits you have accepted or confined yourself within. Who, and what you are is never complete; you are the most fascinating work in progress; a self-aware Rembrandt navigating the cosmos, discovering, tuning, and toning your gifts as the universe calls you home. Be bold, brazen, beautiful, humble, gentle, and kind. Acknowledge the spiritual and physical source of your gifts. Recognize strengths where others perceive weakness; potential in a lost cause; hope in a flickering flame with just enough gusto to help another navigate the great weight of fear, loss, and doubt.

(rembrandt)

No matter the season, the river finds a way to flow; in that regard, it is always home. If the pace of the river will not be deterred, perhaps it is us who must learn to slow down? Comforted by the sound of water in motion, relentless like the tides of the ocean. We mustn't be swift to be steady, nor fast to convey endurance to last. Like the tortoise who finds freedom in its leisure, look to nature and let her be your teacher. What hurry is this world in, to arrive at a destination unknown? Why are we holding onto such pervasive fear, from which decaying ill-nature is grown? Our time here will come to pass, only memories of how we treated others, and what we offered to the world will last. Like the turning leaves which burst into color before letting go and falling from the trees, there is beauty in our passing, and blessing in descending to the earth; enriching the soil from which we've grown. *Our voices echo in the ripple of eternity, if we retrace our origin, by charting our stars.* Like these falling leaves alongside the river, your vibration and ability to shine your true colors, is the guiding light for another to find their way home. But to shine, we must flow; and to flow, we must let go of what's heavy. It's alright if you're not ready or don't even know what it means to be; your time will come. Be quiet, be still, and remember our friend the tortoise: authentic, slow, steady.

(slow and steady)

Too often, I see myself for what I am not. We are conditioned to focus attention on what we lack, rather than appreciating what we are, and what we have. If we are unable to recognize the blessings which constitute our being, inadequacy will be the lie we spend forever believing. Seeing yourself in a positive light requires honesty, practice, and reflection. It demands the same commitment and energy that you expend condemning your faults, flaws, and shortcomings. It asks for you to be gentle and mindful when taking inventory of your quality, careful not to overlook your best parts. You are complex, but you are not an equation that can be reduced to any of its parts or pieces. *Make an effort to remember your strengths with the same intensity as you scrutinize your shortcomings. Effort is a readily available and accessible sign of love.* We have the unique ability to transform weakness into strength. We are ever-changing beings whose potential knows the power of a thousand horses. Only your fear and resistance to your resilience can deter your river from flowing. Lift the floodgates and embrace a destination unknown; knowing you are growing; knowing you are home.

(what i am)

Our heartbeat is our home. Breath, chemistry, and joy dictate its pace. Listen to its lessons, honor its sacred space. Uniquely tuned to your song, sing it to the world before your time is gone. For those afraid of wearing it on their sleeve, remember the sequoia has no fear of being a tree; and miracles cease to be without belief. Even a healthy heartbeat rises and falls, let joy be your compass, sail in every direction it calls. Love is the oxygen your heart needs to breathe, passion is your pulse, guiding you towards all you really need. Fill your home with people, activities, and experiences which lift you, compelling your gratitude for every breath you breathe. Find those with kind, wide eyes to harmonize your song. Be the reason a friend learns to sing their ow n. Let the beat of your heart always be a reminder that when you're true to yourself, you're already home.

(your song)

I wrote my first love song and didn't know it was about you. When you close your eyes, what is it you see? I imagine it to be a loving, hopeful world, learning from and leaving widespread fear and misery. What makes your heart beat? Is it the rush of colliding energy at its precipice in city streets, or is it your time along streams, among trees, gazing under the stars you sleep? I've found we don't receive answers to questions we don't seek. Which songs do you wish to sing? If forced to abandon your home in a fire, which one thing would you bring? Do you want to be wed in a church or on a beach? When you read books what knowledge or comfort do you seek? When you sleep, what is it that you dream? Are you faithful of what's to come, or skeptic until it is seen? I sing these questions into the world, hopeful one day soon you will hear their tune. I speak these intentions from my heart, because I have always worn it on my sleeve. I am finding you with my words, because they have always led the way; and when it is to you — with you — I'll always stay.

(these questions)

This is the adventure of me. An adventure at sunset, where light today tangoes with darkness that delivers tomorrow. The ongoing balance between familiar truth, and the coming lessons we grow to know, and borrow. We recognize our own; we discover home in all places, people, and phenomena in which we see ourselves. Gaze into ineffable beauty and feel its gaze stirring forth in you, with you, because of you. Be the tide, moved by the moon, under the shooting stars. Embrace the inevitable motion known as constancy and change; be grateful for and demonstrate accumulated wisdom gifted with age; fall asleep in love with your story, and the certainty of knowing you shall wake tomorrow to turn another page. You are the reason you're moved by spectacular beauty and pain; you are the season that never fades, nor gives way, unless you deny your potential to change. You are rage, you are peace, you are tyrants brought to their knees. You are here you are now; you are past you are present; you are king, queen, servant, you are peasant.

(the adventure of me)
Inspired by Rob Riccardo

Love and guidance enter through the heart. While I'm getting better at surfing the waves of emotion, and the potency of a swell's magic or destruction, there are times when I'm reminded of my own vulnerability. In these weary moments I tell myself to allow space for them, observe them, and better understand the full spectrum of my soul's intention. It is clear to me that my emotional spectrum and capacity are an instrument from which I am to help others, navigate their own. I have learned to build better boundaries, and embrace the freedom of solitude that my mission requires. Within my soul are the instructions to answer the call. It comes from a place beyond my travels, yet well within my understanding. It encompasses me at all times, as either friction insisting I retrace my steps to once more find the way, or as an infinite series of reaffirming omens giving me permission for the modes and matters within which I discover joy.

(instrument)

I might not know you yet, but the best things come from where you didn't expect. Rising with the sun, growing myself in all the places where there was neglect. Slowing down, to pick up speed; leveling up for those in need. Deeper breaths, to connect; trust in how I feel is real; reality is a reflection of my perception of the good in others, and spirit that moves. Motion beside the vibrating ocean reminds me that the ingredients to the potion have always resided deep within my soul. A unique but common piece of the puzzle, helping others find their way home. Take ownership of the ingredients in your recipe; practice the habit of creating with the intent to share until it becomes necessity. Tuning my instrument so I can help you carve yours from a block of wood, given to you by the earth. Let our collective efforts resemble the poetry of an orchestra, committed to the eloquent practice of its mutual love rehearsed.

(ingredients)

We live in a world competing for attention, swaying us with bells and whistles in every direction; telling us what to choose, what we'll lose, prescribing a daily regimen for how we oughta be used. Each of us has a different answer to where we look for hope when a loved one is diagnosed with cancer, lost at sea to addiction, or when the weight of cold water instills affliction, seemingly too heavy to bear. We wear problems as if they were only our own, how is it on a planet with eight billion people we can feel so damn alone? Maybe in a world of products it's time to fight back by choosing people. I don't just mean the ones we wed in a church and steeple; but the choice to care and let go of ego; lend a hand; hold a hug; and not fool ourselves into believing help needs to come from above; when we know it comes from love, sacrifice, and really just fucking being nice! Which is natural by the way.

Today might be a good time to try it; call it a new way to diet. Most of you always have, and always will; while others are still looking for it in a pill because a guy named Bill continues to pass his own agenda in a House, that is anything but a home, filled with representatives few of us really know. Stifling hope, serving few and not many; squeezing life out of a lifeless penny; dividing the conquered; conquering the divided; flipping a system with the illusion it is two sided. Selling scarcity under the guise of capitalism, when abundance is provided.

(hold a hug)

You've toured for three decades... gloriously. What are some anchors you've utilized to keep the fire ignited and stay focused on your passion?

Yeah, we've been at it for three decades. What do I use to keep focused on my passion? I keep listening. I always try to get new stuff in my ears and see what music can do in different contexts. I long to mirror that and play all kinds of music; I love all kinds of stuff. New content in those forms always fires me up and keeps me going, wanting to recreate that stuff in a context that people are dancing and having a good time. Also, I like to throw in some political messages; messages about love and bringing it all together. The direction our culture needs to go because music needs to do that too. That's what keeps me fired up; trying to spread the love of music and having that affect our culture. That's a mission.

—Vince Herman, Leftover Salmon

Perhaps what you're looking for is also looking for you? Home in coffee shops, concerts, coastlines, and Great Lakes. Letting abundance in, letting go of mistakes. Shedding the days behind, embracing fate. Allowing dreams to find you, se la vie to the chase. Treasure these times to manifest even better upon the horizon; one day you'll hardly believe what you're fixating your eyes on. The love in you is magnanimous; your patience poetic; your joy prophetic; your consistency, alphabetic. To be foundational and sequential, building but never breaking; generous, yet so rarely taking. Love is in the making, relieving, seeing, and believing. Faith is in forgiving fracture, rebuilding in the direction of rapture, and finding a way to do it again after it all falls to pieces. These leases on life are uncertain; peer behind the curtain to learn these flames will stop burning, yet the earth keeps turning; so be drawn in the direction of your yearning. Journey with those you are endeared to; treasure your kin. Love with all of your heart, feel deeply, and let the very best in.

(love is)

Momentum is a real and tangible force. If you wish to improve your environment it begins the moment you decide that despite your active or lingering doubt within, you ought to treat others with the love and kindness given to you by those who you hold closest in your heart. Although not all of us will commit it to words, feeling inadequate is woven into human genetics. However, it is a struggle that no man or woman alone has to bear. It is a difficult conversation to have with others because we wish to project the best vision of ourselves to the world around us, but without regularly participating in vulnerability, we allow pride to be the vehicle by which our suffering is delivered. We are human yet our grasp of just what that entails continues to baffle us. It is alright to ponder upon mental or physical deficiencies that accompany you in this life, but I insist that you similarly reflect over the attributes that make you wonderful. Give yourself a chance to conquer the lingering darkness that passes in and out of all of our lives, yet only finds home in those who choose to believe the human spirit will not prevail.

(wonderful)

Struggle and strife are obstacles you must hurdle while pursuing your passion. There is no roadmap to rid you of the wrong turns you are certain to make on your journey; but life is about trying to find significance in each step and turn you take, even if there is none. The reassurance and affirmations you seek will be revealed externally in the eyes, smiles, hearts, and love of the lives you are blessed enough to touch, and be moved by. As the captain, you must steer your ship and ensure you are not swallowed by the sea; but the great ocean is a beast that cannot be tamed and predicted. Remain flexible and focus your attention on the lessons you have learned, holding true to your intuition and imagination.

(intuition and imagination)

I never knew a rainbow that didn't speak to my heart

Aiding my journey to you, whoever, wherever you are

A picturesque sign of alignment

A brief reprieve from the resistance

A portal to another universe not so different

With better timing, greater clarity

Abundant love reciprocated with regularity

Home and permission to belong, shared unsparingly

Growing stronger with each breath

Empowered despite its wear and tear on me

With the power of creator in us

It is only a matter of moments before we're free

Beating hearts, bleeding hearts, magic flowing in our veins

Given new life and revitalized spirit every time it rains

Nothing will ever be the same

An oath to growth, not decay

Better to burn, than fade away

I never knew a rainbow that didn't speak to my heart

Aiding my journey to you, whoever, wherever you are

(an oath to growth)

Not all ships set to sea with a certain course. Accidents have paved the way to our western world. Allow space to consider your mistakes, shortcomings, and resistance to grow are unfolding in divine time, letting you recognize both your need and capacity to grow into your power. I often use trails of breadcrumbs as an analogy or guide, leaving us signs along our path to self-discovery and mastery. We are drawn to that which we are moved by; as such we seek comfort and home in all people, places, and experiences within which we recognize the best pieces of ourselves.

(home in all places)

The color of love

Home in a hug

Faith in foundation

Growth in goodness

Goodness in patience

Patience in practice

Empathy through quality in patience and practice

Becoming by way of discovery

Discovery by way of becoming

Running towards

Building towards

A harmonious force

Guiding our course

Towards smooth sailing

(towards)

CHAPTER 3

DREAMS

Exhale and take solace knowing that even your worst of days, can serve as a catalyst for you to grow and understand the ingredients required for you to experience your very best. You don't have to breakdown to breakthrough, but you can—if and when you choose to love and listen to yourself, your heart, your anxiety, and your perfectly healthy fear— as it guides you back on path to your authentic self. I woke this morning to a torrential downpour and a proper island thunderstorm. Storms and the sea have long been my cadence in the chaos. I enjoyed a cup of coffee in the hot tub as the rain bestowed its blessing and lesson of cycles and process. Like my Mamyte (Lithuanian for mom) so often does, I began my day listening to Paul Simon as we so frequently did during our time together gifted by the pandemic. Having loved Paul Simon well before knowing my aunt Ginger's brother plays percussion in the band, their songs and sounds landed with extra clarity and comfort on this particular Saturday morning on Hilton Head Island in the rain. Lyrics from "Me and Julio Down by the Schoolyard" rang with emphasized resonance:

Well I'm on my way

I don't know where I'm going

I'm on my way

I'm taking my time

Lately I have felt and identified a resistance within myself to slow down, and grow by allowing the reciprocal goodness which I have deposited into this realm to be returned back onto me. Likely as the result of fearing scarcity, when we are always on the move, immediately investing our energy and love into the next task, project, or relationship, stress and strain interferes with our ability to process and recognize our progress.

(resistance)

My trail of breadcrumbs have been guiding me to step into my power and invest my love into telling my story, trusting that its content could be medicine for others along their greatest journey. Yesterday a friend that some of you know as Dixon's Violin told me that whenever Jerry Garcia met an inspiring musician, he asked them "where is your guitar?"

For some time I have been guilty of traveling without my notebook. For some months prior to that I was guilty of traveling with a notebook that I wasn't writing in. No one can realize your dreams for you; gifts are God's greatest blessings, but even the seeds of redwood trees must be watered. Do not be discouraged if you have neglected your calling, because this is me picking up the pieces, and allowing myself to embrace my heart's desires, trusting that doing so will invite the love I seek into my life. Let go of timelines, comparisons, and your regrets, they will not help carry you to your dreams.

(watered)

A good day generally begins in the days previous. Being present is difficult enough without negative energy carrying through the night, into a new morning. When we do not feel like ourselves, we question the choices which led to us feeling as such. I woke today feeling refreshed and grateful for the cool air blowing off the lake, carrying the sounds and smells of nature through my window, into my lungs, into my words. I feel rested after honoring my energy and choosing myself over Hoxeyville (a Michigan music festival that takes place each August in Wellston). Life isn't about navigating between *good* and *bad* decisions, rather trusting your intuition and allowing it to guide you to healthier, better ones which align with your purpose.

Choosing this over that doesn't mean you wouldn't enjoy one or the other. I had been looking forward to Hoxeyville since I booked Jordan Hamilton as an Artist at Large there in February. An Artist at Large performs multiple times, with multiple different ensembles/acts. I was looking forward to reuniting with Dave Simonotte and Trampled By Turtles who I adore, and have formed a working relationship with between the two times we hosted Dave at Otus Supply in Ferndale, MI, and photographing them at The Masonic Temple when they opened for The Avett Brothers in Detroit. I was looking forward to camping with my good friends because I miss them, and often camp/travel alone. Navigating your stars requires an acute understanding of what you want, what you need, and what you can do about it. I have no attachment to being consumed by my love, and passion for music. Instead, I set the intention to make space for all the ways I long to grow. This space breathes oxygen into my wellbeing, and ability to realize other dreams.

(rest)

Talent and positive energy are natural resources like fresh water and forests, both at risk of depletion if their source is not protected and preserved. When we are brought into this world we are given a body as a vessel to carry our heart and soul, but only after living do we learn it must be treated like a temple if we hope not to simply survive, but thrive. This is a valuable lesson that each person learns or lives their life suffering from, yet no matter your trade, it is never too late to seek the balance you need. Just ask Boston-born Ryan Montbleau, who plays more than 200 gigs annually with his band.

"One of the things I forget over the years... I'm a musician, I'm in the business of healing, but one hard lesson that I've really had to learn, and I'm still learning, is that if I don't take care of myself, then I can't take care of other people. I'm thankful for the opportunities that I get to do this and play, and people listen, it's all amazing, it's all a blessing. But if I don't take a break sometimes, and turn inward, and have quiet then I can't get loud and get crazy so that's a big lesson for sure," Montbleau told us following his set at the Gathering of the Vibes.

—Ryan Montbleau

If your dreams are grand (and I hope they are), realization is a dynamic process and journey forged through time and space. This process relies on the help, support, and faith of others to perceive the vision you pursue, along with the mutual understanding that there is space for one another atop the mountain, basking under the sun. Water is one, the way we must remember that we are. No beginning, no middle, no end. Each piece connected to the next; made stronger and more vibrant with the awareness that "I am he as you are he as you are me, And we are all together."

("I Am The Walrus", The Beatles).

Fall in line with your purpose, to fall in love with your path. Walk in the direction you're called. Enjoy the stroll. Embrace divinity. Accept that it's meaningful and necessary. Hone and own your magic. Help others grow theirs. Be someone who cares. Give a shit. Lend a hand. Hold open the door. Ask questions; listen. Smile. Sunset in the mountains. Sunset on the lake. Remember that you are wild. Be wild. Tango with grace. Let it go. Let it grow. Sow with intent. Let those you love vent. Relax. Sweat. Adventure. Trust. Love. Understand what it means. Dream with care. Think of others. Help others. Hold on with hugs.

(dream with care)

I am a keeper of the light. It is a path I willingly choose and embrace, because my days are brighter with its flame. Whether you're lost at sea, or drowning in the darkness of night, we find a way to shine, to be a lifeline with our light. The weight of water builds until it gives, the very way a heart can grow cold until its carrier lives, and lifts others with its gifts. Days grow longer as our song grows louder; our roots lay deeper as we learn to be keepers, of one another's light; along with the decency that protects everyone's access to dream by day, and by night. When my dream, and your dream, become our dream, progress is in sight. *If we embrace the unfamiliar with the energy we expend condemning it, we could learn to burn hate and turn it into better days.* A people who pray for the well being of all people, of all dreams, in times of darkness, in times of light; for all the times a cold world has left us feeling all alone at night. For each other, with each other, first we see, then learn to be, a keeper of the light.

(keeper of the light)

Inspired by Rob Ricaddo

Your good health and by direct correlation your happiness, increases the likelihood that you'll invest your time, and love into caring for another's. When operating from a place of goodness and momentum, we infuse wellness into the ecosystems within which we operate, aspire to, and reside. This osmosis, or energy transfer is the precise exchange which calls us to slow down, recharge, and rest. It is like a drug, insisting that we ground ourselves in nature, and build a foundation onto which we garden, grow, and let go. We must move and process energy the way water is cycled from earth to sky, being absorbed, giving life where it is needed. Stagnant water festers disease; we are water. Move in the direction of your dreams. If it is currently difficult for you to clarify what your dreams are, move in the direction of your joy. Let the smile on or absent from your face be a compass, leading you to people and places you've yet to imagine.

(osmosis)

Do not be discouraged if it is difficult for you to imagine your dreams, let alone them coming true. I imagine seeds grow into trees without ever considering the possibility of not fulfilling their destiny; let us be more like trees. I imagine even during a wildfire, trees utilize their energy to endure rather than deplete their resources worrying if they will burn.

(be like trees)

Energy is either depleted or replenished, depending upon where you apply it. It is abundant but not unlimited; be mindful of whom and where you divide it. Focus your attention where it feels warm and natural. Joy should exude from those who you spend your time with. Make space and sit with those who ignite your spirit. Spend your time with people who offer solutions, encouraging your dreams as something more than illusions. Offer your light to those who reflect it upon others, paying kindness forward. It is healthy to take inventory of who you spend your time with; in many ways we are the company we keep. Joy and happiness come as the result of filling our well within. A bank wouldn't let you make a withdrawal without making a deposit; consider applying a similar concept to those who you share your energy with.

It is natural that we make more time for those who give it back, but the reality is an equation less exact. It's okay to give more than we receive, but happiness is needy and in many cases it isn't healthy to give freely. Protect your spark by surrounding yourself with those who shine; they will magnify your glow and inspire peace of mind. Take note of the people and places who remind you of the magnificent, capable, and powerful being you have always been. Remember, dreams grow from a source deep within, but they require water, sunlight, and conditions - just right.

(protect your spark)

A commitment to carry my words by carrying my notebook. Making space for my gift is the equivalent to feeding logs to a fire. Each of us requires fuel to burn—without it we tap ourselves— draining our spirit and natural flow. What she gives is not endless; nor is our time here. If now isn't the time, what are you waiting for? Are you lacking the tools to carry out the work? Are you still searching for a course to be charted? We tell ourselves that there isn't time, but it isn't true. If you had to take a shit, you'd find time. It feels reasonable that we ought to nurture our dreams with the same necessity as we go to the bathroom. Deferred dreams are likely the reason our nation is so unhappy, fractured, and intent on tearing each other to pieces. Happy people don't consistently mistreat others; they find a way to help empower them because they are tuned into the potency of passion, and what it yields when aligned with – is the universe's currency: an endlessly flowing river which never runs dry.

(feed the fire)

Can you recall a time when a fan or someone who really appreciated your music shared a time when it got them through a really rough time?

Absolutely man – Facebook – one of the really nice things about it is that it really does connect you to people and I see those messages and there have been a lot of them. Fans who express to us that our music got them through a dark time or this certain song has been really meaningful to them. I mean, I cannot think of a more rewarding payoff. Sometimes you spend these long hours practicing, playing, traveling and it feels a little inward sometime. For every hour we're on stage there's fifty hours where we're working on that stuff, traveling to get to the gig, and learning the music and writing the music. So when you have these people telling you these things, it gives you that real honest connection with the person. It's all those things put together that have helped someone out and enriched their life, that's what it's all about.

—Chris Pandolfi, The Infamous Stringdusters

Operating from a place of joy and passion will guide you to the true purpose of your time here. Whether you have acknowledged it or not yet, each of us has a purpose, and said purpose will make a meaningful impact on others' lives. Try thinking of gifts as a duty to serve yourself by serving humanity; which as a result will bring goodness into your life. Helping others is the greatest marketing tool for your unique offering. We live in a society addicted to talking about themselves, and what they can do for others. I understand the value and necessity of being able to clarify and articulate an offering, but we are beings who learn best by example. Therefore it is more effective to engage than it is to explain.

(gifts as duty)

Only you can determine and from there dictate the pace your life ought to be lived at to ensure your wellbeing, happiness, and optimal trajectory. Each of us has so much to learn from our efforts, energy, and wavering enthusiasm. As of late, I have found myself loving live events a little less during a stretch of six consecutive weekends on the road. This doesn't mean that I don't enjoy them, or lack gratitude for my ability to participate and in some instances execute them; rather it became very apparent that I needed to take a break, and be more selective going forward. *More isn't always better*, and if you're not enjoying it either make an adjustment or let it go. We often overlook how much we change on our way to achieving dreams. As we change, what we want inevitably changes along with us. Try not to be the one forcing a fate which longer serves you. Give yourself permission to adjust your sights as you ascend to new heights.

(wavering enthusiasm)

My dreams take me in the direction of people who are like me: those who create, innovate, and prioritize time to celebrate just how magnificent life is. Not with a wish, but with a will and a way, connected by an infinite number of choices made with passion and reluctance to stray. Each day we wake up with the opportunity to build upon the foundation of a lifetime. What is it you wish to build? Can you paint me a picture of how you behold beauty? A snapshot of time you hope to see? Why would we be given the ability to dream, without the reality of some coming true? If you've found your beach, do you seek it? If you're giving love away, are you taking the time to receive it? Can you recall the last time you made a promise to yourself and believed it? Consider all the ways you spend your energy and if you really need it. Our energy is a resource refueled with passion; sheer necessity will inevitably deplete it. Infinity resides deep within, but only you can free it.

(infinity)

To be happy, I must choose to be happy. To choose to be happy, I must choose to participate in the experiences I love. To participate in the experiences I love, I must discover what it is that I love. To discover what it is that I love, I must ask myself what it is that I am passionate for. To discover my passion I must live my life, do, and not simply say. To live my life, I must accept both happiness and sadness, love and pain. To accept these things, I must accept myself and balance the ongoing relationship between free will and fate. Acceptance comes after I take ownership of both my success and misfortune. Things start to improve when we focus on improving ourselves one day at a time. Sleep less (or more), exercise, work smarter, eat healthier, help others, and engage passion. Lives are wasted gazing upon calendars for vacations down the road, weekends to come, and excuses to regress from the person you wish to be. Build momentum and find rhythm by pursuing your passion and that which you really need: health, family, friends, and joy. Quit critiquing your life because of what your internet friends (and strangers) are doing with theirs. You made your decisions, give yourself some credit and stick to them. If you really aren't happy then you've got some work to do. But that's the arrangement.

(the arrangement)

How would we know where dreams take us, if nobody ever chased them? What would we know of faith, if it wasn't required to see? Without worry and tension, how would we grow gifts into blessings, and burdens into lessons? Each of us becomes capable with the choice to believe we're able. No one can make the choice for you, but if you open your eyes you will be given guides, woven together with instinctual sources stemming from a place deep inside. We write poems and sing songs about the soul, yet so few seek the substance that satisfies it. Shiny objects distract us from dreams in the form of desires; water is life yet we utilize alcohol to medicate and mitigate, while it fuels growing fires. Can you harness the positive energy that emits from your flame? Can you retrace your steps to a heart centered place, or have the critters eaten the trail of breadcrumbs leaving you lost in your head for days?

Dreams deferred become lessons learned, as lives with fleeting joy are practiced, but it is never too late to decide to have a hand in your fate, and embark on a journey fueled by faith. *If anything deserves a chance, isn't it your happiness?* Why not chase dreams like we chase romance? Why not ask joy to dance? What if your happiness is the worst that could happen? Seems like it is worth the risk. Wouldn't it be nice to give your dreams a big, wet kiss? Afterall, why else were you making a wish?

(your flame)

Magic is lost in the grind. Do what you love, love what you do — a simple and elegant philosophy —practiced by too few. We place pride where passion resides; dare you live a lifetime without taking a chance on your dreams, following your inner guide? To find your true path you may need to stray from convention, with the invention of purpose from the surplus of ingredients that set your soul on fire. What is your mission with this life? When you wake up in the morning, what do you hope to create with your day? Who helps you transform these hopes into realities? Do you really want the things you say? Or do others want them for you? It is healthy to make space for the changes occurring within our being, by seeing joy in new possibilities for what's to come upon the horizon. This daily flux is fluid; one choice leads to the next — but what we hope for changes — that much you can expect. Each second of the hour holds the power for you to devise your fate, by considering what it is you want to create. Rise and shine with a sense of vigor and purpose; ascribe meaning to every day, otherwise you're giving it permission to be worthless.

(ascribe meaning)

Trust your heart, in time you'll see. Your truth has been within you this whole time — often disguised and doubted by your own mind — but what better a find than the pure substance of your soul? On our way to a happier, healthier union with ourselves, our gifts, our origin, and destination to one another. How good are you willing to let it be? What longing of your soul do you need to acknowledge to be free? What declaration of dreams and pursuit shall you decree? Let joy be the reason this Christmas season. It is time to listen to the hopeful signs provided, and co-create as you are guided. When it comes to your soul's greatest desires, don't you think it's time to give in? Is there a piece of you that has grown cold and quiet? Do you feel the train's leaving the station while you deny it? It's never too late to buy a ticket and take the ride, but guides are more helpful when you know what you wish to find.

(give in)

No one can tell you what to do with your gifts, though they will try. How do you wish to help shape a better world? What do you want this world to keep of you? When you dream at night, where is it that you're taken, and what in your waking hours can you do to get there? Who in your life do you envision, or acknowledge helping you get there? Who and what is holding you back, and what is your attachment to it, and them?

I wouldn't recommend my path to anyone, because it is uniquely tailored to my gifts, joy, and calling. Each of us has access to this divine flow, but no one can decipher its equation for you. Only your heart possesses the roadmap and key to your destiny.

Each of us has the opportunity to be the trail of breadcrumbs which helps another navigate a ladder to their stars.

Stop asking permission, and start asking for what you want.

I'm growing into myself, by being myself.

(being myself)

Find your words and be reminded you have a voice. Take a deep breath and be reminded the path you choose is a choice. Love others and discover the world in return. Wake up, grateful to learn, grow, and tomorrow do it again. Be a friend and discover a lover. Be yourself and begin to understand what that means. Take chances and remind yourself of the dreams hidden behind closed eyes. Try on a smile and see its ability to introduce joy in others. Create community by being a positive rhythm within one. Vibrate in tune with your soul, and harmonize with abundant energies all around. *Remember the good with the same intensity as you scrutinize your shortcomings.* Remember to remember. Remember to let go. Remember to believe in your own love story. Remember to write it every day.

(love story)

Move me moon, so I may move another

Shining on, from above

Shining down, unconditional love

Moonlight shines the same on all faces

Sisters and brothers

Help one another

Moved in the direction of our dreams

Carried by a river no one sees

Lifted by a rising tide

Water flowing through me

Isn't it time?

(direction of dreams)

With the fear life insists, let us retreat to the love in our hearts to guide us towards the love in the world. Let us use the starlight within our soul to navigate to the place of realized dreams and peace. Together we find the cadence of breath, discovering union within practice, balance with being, and believing without seeing. Repeat after me:

Rise and shine, with each breath this day is mine, because it is ours who gaze to the stars, knowing *creation is in our blood, manifested in the name of love*. Rise and shine, now is the time to embrace my destiny, this too shall pass once it's served its purpose testing me. Rise and shine, it is a good day to grow, I have faith and embrace the road to realizing my dreams. Rise and shine with the sun, it is time for a new dawn to illuminate our people to protect our planet. Rise and shine until day grows into night, then burn a candle when you find yourself lost from light.

(union within practice)

One of my favorite lyrics: "If you've got pain in your bones, you know you're not alone." To me, this is about our tendency to isolate ourselves despite our similarities and connections to others... even though we're all subject to a similar struggle. What do you think?

Absolutely, I think that's a great analysis. San Antone is one of our oldest tunes and still one of my favorites to play. Griffin wrote that years before we formed and we have seen it go through so many iterations and phases. Over the six years we've been playing it, I've emotionally connected to it in so many different ways and that's the beauty of it. Building off your idea, it seems the song contains a universal sentiment we share and in the same breath, leaves room for a very personal connection within the commonality. I think that isolation or polarization due to fear, pain or struggle, is the last thing that we need these days and that music can help bridge that gap. I love hearing people sing along with San Antone. It's in those moments I believe it's working, unifying us all in our differences and our similarities. It's unbelievably powerful.

—Max Davis, The Ghost of Paul Revere

Feeling guides intuition

Clarity improves the ability to listen

Love always knows what's missing

Be patient with God's mission

Grateful for the time it is taking

Thankful for magic in the making

Mindful of the subtleties of creation

Careful of who we let bathe in our sparkle

Comforted by solitude and the space between breaths

Let present peace, guide what's next

Let go of what you're told to expect

Let in which you wish to be planted

Intuition plus imagination

Ingredients for dreams granted

(ingredients for dreams)

CHAPTER 4

ACTIVATION

Take a deep breath and let go of your worrying ways. Most people don't know what they want to create with this life of theirs. A lot of people pretend like they do — to the extent that they lecture and prescribe advice and lifestyles to others — all the while their pride is just a mask they wear. A lifetime is all we're guaranteed. Rather than trying to figure out the rest of your life, commit to understanding yourself. What is it that keeps you up at night? What makes you smile? If love was encapsulated in a single activity in your life, what would it be? *The world knows few limits other than the ones we impose on ourselves, and our neglected dreams.* Do not let the miserable, calculated, and ill-spirited define, destroy, or deflate you. There is an immense light inside of you and I so dearly wish for you to let it out. I hope to help you heal; to help you believe; to help you retrace your ladder to the stars; to help you shine as if you were one of them; to remind you to love yourself; and to remind you to remind others to do the same.

When I woke up this morning I did not know that I would be interviewing Mike, or that I would learn of his dad's passing as a result of cancer. Or that I would be compelled to share my own internal fear and struggle resulting from my mother's diagnosis with idiopathic pulmonary fibrosis. Or that I would be so compelled by our conversation to let Mike know that I would include Aqueous as one of the bands featured in my next book. And though I never met his dad Doug, I am inspired by his relationship with his son, and feel like I know him a little better after reading Mike's remembrance on the most recent Father's Day.

As the years go by, I seem to have a different perspective and feeling on my Dad's passing. It naturally becomes a little more distant, but also as life moves on, I feel like he lives on more and more in me as I lay out the framework for the rest of my own life with him in the back of my mind, ever present, in a different kind of way. Sometimes it's simply a feeling of longing to share things with him when I make new music, or reach some cool new achievement in my life that he would appreciate in a way that was very unique to who he was. This very intuitive, intellectual human that was an almost conflicting combination of heart, feeling and soul, critical thinking and science–truly unique and special in every way.

His passing was a crash course in staying grounded to the concept of the finite. To recognize that our journey is short and to try to live our best lives, and love strongly, stay off the fucking internet, see the world, explore, and to do all those things that you would definitely do if you knew your time was near. Which is kind of ironic because certainly, for all we know, it IS – but of course, it's natural to get caught up in life's complexities. Some days it's easier than others to feel in touch with that side of it.

—Mike Gantzer, Aqueous

Fourteen-degree-freeze. Heart is beating with rhythm, coffee is warming my belly, this smile seems reluctant to stray. When I was younger people assumed I was on drugs, over time they learned I'm living on love. My daily Drifter Coffee routine has become sacred. A family feel, community vibe, and wonderful reminder that no matter the weather it's a great day to be alive. Now hold onto it and go outside and consider everything from something beyond your default perspective. Marvel in Michigan's frigid shine. Breathe in its cool, crisp, air and dare to cherish each of your days no less than the last, because what if it was? Our environment plays such an integral role in our being, no reason to keep yourself believing that we need any one season more than the other. Like plants, humans are drawn to the sun, but we are made differently you see. We are capable of not only surviving the tundra but thriving in this time when we rest and make space for personal growth.

It is a time of learning, yearning for the warmth of a fire, conversation, one another, and the potential of building what's to come. It is a unique time in this nation where we must decide who we wish to build a foundation with. A time where we must let our hearts guide us to and away from what feels right and wrong, hoping to collectively sing a song so simple and beautiful, the rest of our tribe worldwide will be compelled to harmonize. More than ever we need to capture the imagination of a people divided, and it begins with you and I. In places like this; on days like this; and it doesn't begin with a wish, rather a warm gesture, helping hand, soft gaze, and inviting smile that suggests that you're the type of person who believes in the soul of a man or woman. Someone who believes in the ingredients underneath. Daring to possess faith without needing to see the fine print. The choice not to flee from, but retreat to one another, and discover the multitude of ways we can make one another's lives better, with our own two hands, two feet, reciprocity, and rhythmic heartbeat.

(drifter coffee)

Rather than spending time dwelling over the way you make money, reflect over that which you are best at. What can you contribute that no one else can? What is it you wish to leave behind? When you close your eyes and picture the oration of your eulogy at your funeral, what story do you wish to be told of your physical life passed? *Purpose resides deep in our bones, but we must ask ourselves the right questions to conjure their realization.* Do not be afraid of asking yourself the difficult, meaningful, or neglected questions. It is your destiny to understand, embrace, and harness the greatest version of yourself and purpose.

(neglected questions)

Winter has arrived with snowfall heavy and bright, all through the day and into the night, on the eve of the full moon. Cars are buried, trees freshly powdered; the time has come for collective release, let go and embrace its power. Experience floods my blood, realized in the feel of emotion; after all - the moon moves more than just the ocean. Allow yourself to be moved in whichever direction your heart desires; let these moments be the kindle to help ignite your fire. If you feel it deep in your bones, know you're not alone, and it's about time to let your best intentions show. Without the ability to know where they will go, we plant the best pieces of ourselves into this earth and garden their growth. What are you drawn to most? What pulls you with the allure of the coast? What oath have you wished to make with yourself, yet let slip through the cracks? It's alright, don't look back, don't you worry, slow down and take a breath, there is no hurry. There is only time and space: a living whiteboard for you to create, manifest, and test the limits of your will and wonder. Doesn't it feel like it's time to discover the pieces of you, shining brightest, reflected in the joy and smiling eyes of others? You have the ingredients because you are the ingredients; you are the magic, but still must wave the wand.

(winter whiteboard)

Heavy chest

Shortness of breath

Doing my best

To feel myself again

Breathing deep

Losing sleep

Time to retreat

To myself again

We do our best not to grow cold, tired, and weary

We try to hold onto the flame

Without burning our fingertips along the way

Learning to live

Learning to love

And learning to let go

Making space for something worth holding onto

(myself again)

Running into rhythm. Eager to discern the discipline required to ensure my fire burns. Learning to strum the strings of the cello deep within the bellows of my heart. I am a song written to be sung, and held onto when joy is active and fleeting. I am the words you've been telling yourself but needed to see them in a different light to believe in. I am the doubt behind your eyes and permission to let it go. I am an exercise of faith, endurance, and willingness to learn. I am a twist and turn of fate in your favor. A labor of love and harborer of hugs. Dancing feet and the courage to be what you need, to see dreams woke into reality. Exhaled breath from the chest, into better being; believing what we're seeing, and trust in what remains unwritten.

(unwritten)

Clouds can mask a sunrise like the lies hidden behind a disguise. But truth is light, and will find its time to shine before night; be yours and embrace the sight of power reclaimed. Magic is hidden within you, be yourself and live into its name. Across the ocean birds soar north, south, east and west, aligned with shifting winds, in harmony with what's coming next. Ready, willing, able, and patient enough to experience the edge before fearing what awaits on the other side. I am the ocean, I am the sun, I am the moon, and I am the wind blowing me in their direction. To honor them, I must honor myself and the substance of my soul. Its origin story is written with love, knowing, and invisible ink, like a forgotten vessel, sunk to the bottom of the sea. It calls to me when I am beside it, like a hero's destiny in ancient Greek mythology. I am drawn to its motion and poetry because it is a reflection of a piece of my soul that I know better than words can describe. To honor it I must first honor what is inside, remove my mask, face and embrace the light without disguise.

(without disguise)

Seasons provide space and time to breathe life into the places within which require the most energy to grow. Winter can be a tough time everywhere, but especially in Michigan, because it demands we look inward, and address the faults in our own foundation. I'm not saying we need frigid, tough months to lead us on this journey of a lifetime, but I believe it's something to the effect of addition by subtraction. The busyness of the grind requires such immense energy and attention, especially during pandemic times, that we grow accustomed to habits that do not serve our higher selves, nor enable us to show up to serve others in the capacity we hope to. It is from this duality these words are written, as I navigate the hindrance, and resistance I impose on my personal progress and evolution. But, as a friend recently told me, self-awareness is a good thing, and if you're having these conversations with yourself, these longings to grow in all the ways you're both able, and called to, it's a good sign, and a necessary part of your process. As always, I'm sharing these sentiments to better hear them myself. *Be kind, nurturing, and committed to better supporting your foundation, so it becomes more natural to offer others the same.*

(winter conversations)

These bleak winter days

Call for the most practice

When there are the least distractions

Blanketed in stillness and gray

A gentle calm, a gentler way

These are the days

We learn to better listen

For our true mission

Soul's guidance

A transmission

Through the heart

Within the gap between breaths

It might not be what you expect

Or maybe you've always known

Home is the direction you're called in

Each of us has a calling

Sparks fly when we're all in

(transmission)

Wake up believing that you're right on pace, right on time, and even your kindest measurements of yourself are tricks of the mind. A snapshot cannot reveal the being you've grown to be, the storms you've weathered and learned to flee, nor the potential for all things which you've planted like seeds, growing into a tree with leaves of all sizes, shapes, and colors. You are not your best or worst moment in time, rather a circular line that harmonizes the sound of a thousand voices, born from a thousand choices which paint a picture of the road you've traveled, but cannot determine the direction your journey will unravel. Each day, each breath, comes with a compass pointing north, south, east, and west, quiet the voice in your head and feel for the beat of the heart within your chest. It is your map, instinct - your key. These days are your days, to be directed by your gaze. Focused attention in any direction, will yield evidence of your intentions.

(your gaze)

I want you to embrace that you can lift yourself up. You can help yourself out. You can remind yourself to smile. You can make yourself laugh. You can remember how to love yourself. You can lift others from darkness and despair. You can offer others a helping hand when they appear to have none. You can give someone a reason to smile who hasn't had one in a while. You can inspire laughter in someone who needs it even though they won't ever let you know. You can help others recognize the love already in their lives. You can help others learn to help themselves. You are the difference. You possess the power of one. You are the leader this world needs. You are the key to the kingdom we seek. You are our hope. You are our dreams. You are the person we wish to see when we look in the mirror each morning. Close your eyes, open your heart, take a deep breath and live extraordinarily! You can do it, we believe in you. Carry yourself with enthusiasm and pursue your passion with confidence and conviction. Carry yourself so you can prepare to carry others. Carry hope so it may be passed to those who one day follow in our wake.

(you can)

Helping hands hold humanity together, piece by piece, brick by brick. Small, subtle miracles are the glue we take for granted, the fortune we fail to realize we've been handed — opportunity as a result of others' good will — we've been granted. The tendency to reduce ourselves induces scars that we're left to carry. But scars tell a story like the stars paint the night sky. Embrace their lessons, and observe their beauty. Dare to see more in yourself than you did the day before. Walk through the doors others are kind enough to open; be the relief and solution for which others are hoping. Given two hands: One to hold, and one to help. Given a heart beat, to give a shit. Given life to live, not to quit. Pick up the pieces so we help others learn to do the same. Two steps forward, one step back - progress is a process, not quite exact. Hang in there, you must be getting close. Hang in there, others need you more than you know. Learn to love yourself as much as you love others, doubt is a great weight to tow. Quit reducing yourself, you know how hard you've been working to grow. It's a good day to give yourself some credit, by cutting yourself some slack. No matter the narrative and timeline in your head, you're right on track.

(trust the process)

Today, you walk with extra pep in your step, confidence in yourself, and joy in your laugh. Today, you start giving the same effort towards believing in yourself that you have long spent reducing yourself. Today, you will continue your journey towards lifting the spirits of others, because you have taken the necessary time and commitment to lift yourself. Today, you serve as an inspiration to others for your positive outlook and gentle nature. Today, your laugh will heal wounds of others who have long forgotten the feeling of their own laughter. Today, you will help others believe that they are not, and will not, ever be alone in this. Today, you are the good sign your friend, neighbor, and even enemy are looking for in the world. Today, you stand tall and will inspire such integrity and posture in those who have been weighed down by the perpetual pressure, and challenge of gravity. Thank you for helping us carry on.

(why not you?)

In these winter months we must look our choices in the eyes, and see the person we have become. There is no denying the experiences that have come to pass, delivering us to this very moment in our evolution. An individual can intend to do all things, but we will not be remembered by our best intentions. There is no running from the person you have become, and with time-ticking one wonders why anyone would ever want to flee from his or her potential? If you find it difficult to swallow the choices and actions you have made, then perhaps it is time to be the person you have always intended. If you're looking for an excuse, an opportunity, permission, or a sign, look no further. Cold winds blow even colder for those hiding in plain sight. Whether you'd like to admit it or not, you are the architect of your reality and no one will build it for you. Let freedom be a blessing and not a burden; a catalyst for all choices you failed to make but wished to. Allow yourself to be inspired by your desire to contribute to the wellbeing of our species.

(permission)

Success is not a means to measure yourself with the world around you; and personal success is not contingent on the efforts of others. Why do we measure ourselves against the progress of others, when their paths could not be more dissimilar than our own? Give yourself a break and believe in the choices you have made. Give yourself some credit and accept that along the way you likely made the best decisions you could, with the information available to you at the time. Give yourself a chance to be the person you once saw in your dreams, realizing your full potential in the very way you felt was honest to your set of unique skills, and intricacies. The world will give you plenty of reason to reconsider and doubt; stand in your corner and practice gratitude for those standing by your side. No person is an island.

(honest)

You talk about the worst thing that ever happened to you being the envy and negative thoughts you had towards other musicians who were achieving commercial success, then those very same musicians were there for you when you got sick, and threw your benefit shows. What advice do you have for other musicians who find themselves defeated by negative thoughts and envy along their way to success?

Well, it's not always easy but you just have to take your mind and your attitude to – why did you play music? What attracted you? I mean, what is it? And the love of the music, but it's not always easy to remember that and you can get disillusioned. I had fallen into a trap. It was about '81-'82, and we, the New Grass Revival, had spent two years with Leon Russell. Our visibility was raised, and I just couldn't understand why the rest of the world wasn't catching on to us, you know? So I found myself being envious of other people's position in the world of show business—not their music—we were never envious of other people's music; I knew we had good music.

Maybe it was affecting my attitude a little bit because I felt we deserved it too, but it was quite humbling when yes – in the fall of '82 I was diagnosed with cancer and lo and behold some of the very people I'd become envious of were the very ones who were the first ones to say: "What do you need? We'll throw benefits. We'll help you out. We'll bring you groceries," and that was quite humbling. It shouldn't have taken being that sick to realize that your friends would help you, but it really drove it home. "Come on man, if you can't be happy for your friends, then you're a very small person."

What I learned was that I'm happy for my friends: "Good luck to ya!" If you can't stand and applaud them, then come on, get with it here. I had this leg kicked out from me for a little while and it helped me realize that we're here to help each other, so hopefully I've been able to give back some to them too.

—Sam Bush

Misery loves company. It's your right to be miserable, but own it, embrace it; discover the origin of your misery, and seek to free yourself from it. If you're unhappy you can blame everyone and everything in the world around you, and stay miserable, or you can ask yourself what it is that is making you miserable? Is it your job? Is it the regret of giving up on an idea or dream you once had, or found great passion in? It's never too late to be happy. Every waking moment is another opportunity to change everything that you dislike about your life; but it takes gumption, and courage. Rearranging your plans doesn't mean that you're giving up, or giving in. We were created to be flexible beings capable of adaptation, adjustment, and audibling as the world around us prompts us to do so. One of the greatest realizations that I stumbled upon was that dreams are rarely realized in their original conception. Adjust, make space, and resume pursuit.

(rearrange)

Doubt may rival belief as the most prevalent presence in your life. Struggle is like cancer, and perpetuates doubt like wildfire if not mindfully opposed. Who and what is it that you live for? We must remind ourselves why we wake up each morning, what it is that we love, have endured, and are capable of. Without faith in ourselves, we begin to lose our identity and even the mountains we've climbed, begin to appear as mere mistakes. External doubt will be plentiful. Do not be a source of resistance. Believe in yourself when it is most difficult. Remain in your corner because it is going to be a fight. We all need as much help as we can get.

(wildfire)

This goes out to each of you who is finding a way to shine in a time of woe. To each and every being who is helping another carry the weight; motivated by the smile on their face. We are kind, we are warm, but we are also tenacious, we are also savage. Let pain and suffering be your guide to better days, and a better way, fueled by love. This is for those who practice patience as a prescription for perpetual ignorance. For those whose grace grows with a commitment to find cadence in the chaos. Those with hands worn and bloodied, by building a beacon of tangible hope, to help our tribe find their way to one another; on even the darkest of days. We can do this because we were built for this. With a collective and conscious deep breath, we will be reminded that it is our endurance that ensures we may flourish. Flow into deep seeded places of hate and hurt; planting joy, good will, and the growing notion that we are in this together; no matter the weather; it is time to dance: rain or shine; tingles down the spine; a heartbeat to hold; a dream no longer deferred; all children born with a chance to fly; free as a bird.

(rain or shine)

Guide me spirit with faith in my heart. I am ready to go to a place I have never been, with love I've never allowed. You have blessed me with great wealth and community, while the reciprocated love of one eluded me. Waiting for me to learn to better love myself. You have given me time to find clarity in my heart and mind; you have given me faith, testing me in sacred space; illuminating life's gifts and true treasures—happiness shared— not measured. Thank you for your patience and presence, it has reconnected me to source and reaffirmed a course that brought my gifts to light. Activating me in the good fight for what is heartfelt, what is decent, and what feels right. I am ready for the blessing of entanglement; inspired with the joy of beginning anew, with plans rearranged for two; loving harmony divinely tuned. Great goodness awaits us in this place between the stars and earth. Trust your deep intuition and longing to signify your worth; you are a blessing, not a curse. *Love will lift you when you let it. Faith will find you when you ask for it. Your path will call you when you choose it is time to listen.* The sun will shower you with grace, can you feel it glisten? Take small steps, trust what is given. Believe intuitive vision, and humbly accept God's mission.

(this place between the stars and earth)

Faith over fear. Love takes me where I want to go. Love lifts me to the people and places I am yet to see. Routine is the groundwork of a strong foundation. Routine requires commitment over time. Faith offers me glimpses of what could be mine; along with the reminders of what already is. Source offers a trail of breadcrumbs in the form of signs. They won't all be good, but each will be a lesson. It is a fascinating time to learn and remember your love for learning. Devour wisdom with an oath to growth. Not as a means of comparison or competition, rather clarity and repetition. Lending myself to the growth I know I need, to access the shared abundance we all seek. Letting the river bathe over me, raising my vibration by reducing my hesitation to trust my inner guide. Trust the narrative that leads you and lifts others; but know it is not your duty to carry their weight. When it is your thoughts weighing you down, work on letting them go, and finding your way to better ones. Integrity and intention guide our ascension, while faith, love, and repetition encourage its retention. Inspiration is the beginning of my journey; a spark I am given. My commitment to its continued practice, growth, and possession, reveal my reasons for living.

(devour wisdom)

The water speaks loudly on these mornings

Southeast winds howl

Carrying winter with them

Blowing the last of the leaves from trees

To help blanket the earth

Ripple after ripple

Wave upon wave

Greater enthusiasm for warmth on these days

Thankful for fleece blankets

And the different stages our journey takes us

Daylight retreats for a few more weeks

The earth heals, as should we

Embrace sleep, it's something we need

Feed your fire, to warm from your flame

Pour love into wounds, to ease your pain

Growth means never being the same

Transformation requires change

Be thankful for these days

Saying goodbye to the person you were

Welcoming that which you've become

Joy knows all seasons

Love is the reason

(when daylight retreats)

It is a conscious choice to see the world as mundane, or magical. Your collection of choices over time designs the lens through which you gaze. Praying without practicing, is hoping without hustling. Judgment without journey, is opinion absent of experience. We don't decipher beauty from pain, rather we acknowledge the presence of one within the other. Loss teaches us to let go. Love teaches us to lose gracefully. Joy reminds us not to flee from feeling, while fear fools us into disbelieving; yet faith fills our hearts with the gift of seeing. Whether you like it or not, you see what you choose to; attract what you offer; and embrace what you deserve. Every day can be a journey, and it only *feels* like you're alone. We are connected; activated when aligned; in tune, throughout space and time. We are mundane; we are magical; we are the river; we are the road; we are the leap between zero and infinity.

(the leap)

The ripple of these waters cool the chambers of my beating heart, reflecting the beauty I see in the world, that I'm working on better accepting in myself. Not from a distance or certain angle, shimmer, or hue, rather the transcendent true and through. Like a bird that trusts its wings from first flight, facing my shadow to embrace its contrasting light, figure, and form: thunder to my lightning, in an ocean storm. Be worn but do not be weary. If water is wave, then wave is water, and the distinction between the two is as futile as the effort of attributing the sky, as any single hue of blue. I am equally the pieces of me that I can and cannot change, but my attitude towards the latter is the matter in the darkness of the shadow I face. I rise with the sun to embrace the exchange of equal and opposite forces, with the beauty of a band of horses: running to and away from both darkness and light, with hope in sight, heavy legs and heavy breath, grateful for the ripple of these waters, and the lessons their reflections will show me next.

(first flight)

Memories can haunt us, but that is only because we know how often they carry us: through difficult times, through our loneliness, through the doubt that we may deny from being there at all. Doubt is written in our genetic code. It is planted like a seed from the moment we walk, talk, rise, and fall. Do not be defeated when you bleed. We bleed because we are human; because we can heal, and because we sometimes need to. *We get what we need when we need it, and we bleed because we're human, don't be defeated.* Doubt is our challenge to be the person we believe we can be. It requires a stand: a physical and emotional response. An awareness that we must not remain static or we will devolve. Evolve or fade away. Be better in every way you're called to. We become better, not as a result of wanting to be better, but by being itself. Start small, and grow from there.

(because we're human)

Too soon we forget that it is from struggle that phenomenon is born. Not ashes to ashes, but from ashes to the light of the phoenix. We must allow ourselves to be grounded to this great earth by our uncertain path, pain, and temporary maddening in the face of darkness, panic, and shortness of breath. Too soon we forget that we only live one life; who are we to live free of the world's weight on our shoulders? It is the journey through the depths of darkness that inspires awe as we bask in the euphoric glow of the sun on our face, atop the mountain they said couldn't be climbed; or at least not by the likes of you.

(ashes to light)

.

Great books that tell the stories of better men and women, are not written about those who stumble from man to majesty overnight. Our souls cannot be taxed, gain interest, nor be deterred; but our souls can be measured by an enduring spirit that claws, scratches, and fights its way from worn knees to two feet; standing before the world, accepting nothing short of another breath lived in pursuit of love, excellence, and even the smallest chance to leave behind a story of their own that inspires a better world; inspires a soul broken and beaten by another man's conception of what this life ought to be.

(taxfree)

Stars shine on even the darkest of nights. Their luminescence is present without detection; like the goodness in your veins it prevails without recognition; like the righteousness in your soul it endures independent of measurement; and like the overwhelming abundance of courage in each and every heavy breath, it offers hope in its absence. Goodness is abundant, but until we choose to recognize it in ourselves, we will continue to overlook it in the world around us. Those who commit to loving themselves, pursuing their passion, and the citizen he or she is capable of becoming, will blaze a trail for others who seek a path of alignment. No matter the courage or weariness in your heart, helping hands, shared vibrations, and true community are the best medicine. The plight of struggle will disable the most familiar routine, and while its weight may seem to take every bit of breath from your lungs, there is an undeniable force for good in this world, capable of combating any and all opposing forces. With strength in spirit, strength in numbers, and strength in each other, there is medicine for the people.

(medicine for the people)

While the word "medicine" is perceived in the Western world as medical treatment, prescriptions, and dependence, the American Indians adopted the word in the sense of "magical influence." Forgiveness offers an opportunity to remove one's self from his or her immediate pain and suffering, and transcend to a higher plain where struggle is recognized as an opportunity for growth.

That's funny you ask that because I was just talking to my Filipino family who were trying to teach me to say Medicine for the People in Tagalog. One way means drugs, one means healing. If you are into food, plants, medicine, earth stuff, your understanding of medicine is different than Western medicine. Western medicine conjures a certain idea... We're offering a cool, revolutionary way to talk about music. Music can be healing. That's the thing about words; they have so many meanings.

—Nahko Bear, Nahko And Medicine For The People

Pain is evidence of what you can leave behind when you let go. Why judge the process without learning the ways it helped you grow? Sometimes our course is corrected because our pace needs to slow. Self-care sharpens the needle from which your fruition is sown. Wildfire ignites as we embrace struggle as the catalyst for dreams deferred. There is a candle that each of us needs to light. Upon it, a flame each of us must protect. Surrounding it: darkness to be illuminated. Within it — the potential for peace — or destruction. I believe we are designed to create; governed to be afraid; and measured against one another's best and worst memories. We are blown in the wind; moved by humanity; crippled by it; hopeful because of it; hopeful despite it.

(course correction)

Brick by brick, piece by piece, we pave our way toward a world that embraces peace. Not simply as a blessing at the dinner table, rather an existential and political philosophy from which we live. From the ground up we build upon those who have given their lives, love, and every last breath so we can all remember what it is we've forgotten: We're in this together. Like pieces of an infinite puzzle, shaped and sized uniquely, randomly, perfectly, and poetically. We find our way to one another through creation, connection, community, and unity. Distracted by each other's unique beauties, we forget that beauty of one, is beauty of all, and happiness of one, helps lay the groundwork for the happiness of all. *We are not at war with anyone but ourselves and our planet, and I assure you we can win neither.* It is in our DNA to help each other. Helping others is accompanied by a great magnetic force, emitting fortuity for those trailblazers riding its wave: riding the rhythm of positive vibrations, permeating the metaphysical force from which we came to be. So I say to thee: ride on! Find your rhythm, find your joy, find your wave and ride it into the great beyond. You are curious, you are capable, and you can be courageous in your pursuit of the dreams which sleep behind your closed eyes, without compromising your ethics and integrity. Seek the world, and find it seeking you in return.

(ride on)

A united species is a powerful and pervasive force that our planet has never known. We are similar, yet beautifully unique. Ultimately, we seek the same setting sun upon the horizon, experience joy as a result of the same longings, and suffer as a result of the same traumas. If we begin to hold ourselves accountable, rather than scapegoating our happiness, it will reveal the thought processes and actions which are not acceptable, inspiring growth from fires that breathe below. It will not be scrutiny but empathy that helps facilitate another's growth and evolution; bringing us closer to a common understanding of health, and happiness. Consider the burden of another's pain and suffering, before you pick them apart because of it. Offer to help before contemplating why someone needs it. Start showing up for yourself so you can be present for others. Address your fears and trauma so that you can heal, while helping others do the same.

(showing up)

Ever connected

Ever charged

Ever flowing

Potent, indivisible motion

Undivided

Unafraid

Unapologetic

Untamed

Unarmed

Under, above, within

Flexible

Free

Fluid

(Water)

Tears are a water sacrifice for days and nights filled with the warm embrace of love. Offered in joy, sadness, and gratitude for the ability to form relationships which evoke their release. Every tear is a memory, and every memory is a reminder of the blessings we've been given, and reasons we love living. Our water composition suggests that shedding tears is our way of offering a piece of ourselves to the legacy of those reasons, people, and memories. The tears we shed require vulnerability, and in certain instances suggest the type of person who is offering them. *We must know love, to know loss, and it is the only currency worth the cost.* Meaningful connection and creation with another soul is the reason we are given life. Our love and support of one another leaves imprints beyond our ability to conceive, believe, or measure. Loss is inevitable; but it is also a reminder of the love flowing through our veins, and those who have helped carry our well-being along the way. Embrace the wisdom of your tears, and consider letting them lead you on a journey inward, taking inventory of the blessings and lessons their legacy has left you with.

(water sacrifice)

Like trees shedding leaves, we must let go of our burdens. But before we can let them go, we must take a walk with them and identify where they are showing up in our lives, thoughts, and feelings. As wind moves ripples through water, burdens and trauma condition patterns which influence the way we perceive ourselves, and others. Identifying these patterns, along with the source of their presence is essential in our choice to let them go. Similar to the offering that falling leaves provide the earth for future growth, letting go of painful experiences, relationships, and harmful perceptions will help free us from their weight, making space for the light, wisdom, and love we let in. Like trees shedding leaves, this process makes us vulnerable, but we must face what we fear to better understand its origin story, and how to be free of it. Piece by piece, and leaf by leaf this space is filled with belief, trust, and revelation of the most elegant design. As we begin to better understand ourselves, and the role our past plays patterning the present, we grow more patient with the ability to recognize these patterns in others. It is easier to understand someone when we know the source of their spectacle, but it isn't necessary if we remember that each of us is at a different stage on our healing journey, and everyone will benefit from a little more forgiveness.

(most elegant design)

When we slow down and let healing in, we grow increasingly aware of all of the places and spaces where we could better show up. It's like asking the question you've neglected, because you were afraid of the answer. But once you ask the first question, your fear begins to fade, replaced by the work and commitment required to grow. It becomes more difficult to neglect or be naive of your well-being, which in turn improves your consideration and respect of others' wellness. Water isn't a substance we drink when we're thirsty, it is a blessing and the foundation of our existence which we require at all times. Wellness isn't something we strive for when ill, rather the peace we need to best operate and flourish. Healthy habits are the building blocks for healthy choices, while mindfulness weeds our garden of its excess, making space for our magic to multiply. Wellness knows rhythm like a pure shooter does on the basketball court: feed your healthy habits like you'd feed a hot shooter, and be sure to keep giving them the ball. You won't always be dialed in, hot, and flowing, but these habits help you return to form with added grace and haste, each time you stay.

(added grace)

Winter winds, move through the lake

The way spirit moves through us, when we pray

By acknowledging its presence, we allow its gifts

When we align with, the guidance it gives

Recognizing where - happiness lives

It comes from doing our best

Showing up the way we're able

Bringing our magic to the table

Dynamic, yet stable

Love, flowing where it is called to

Faith, in the direction it is called in

Comfort, in the joy it inspires

Trust, in the reasons it's needed

Sacrifice, for all the times we bleeded

Humility, for the ego we feeded

Patience, because good things take time

Empathy, because who couldn't use a good cry?

Practice is prayer made by our hands and feet

The precipice where intentions and investments meet

Rubber is to road, as compassion is to humanity

(doing your best)

Like growth, healing isn't something we graduate from. It is perpetual; it is a long winding path which pushes us to, and away from others. Navigating your personal path to a higher calling is better supported by those who acknowledge, and practice ascension of their own. Our ability to rise from conditioning and circumstances with the knowledge in our hearts that we have gifts, and with those gifts we are called to better serve one another with compassion and love. Naturally, it is difficult to be in service of others when your airplane is enduring turbulence, and you fear you're about to crash. This is why we must take the steps to heal.

(higher calling)

With our words we will change this world by understanding what it means to be a part of it. Everyday we me must work on taking better care of ourselves, so we are open to, and moved by helping others.

Everyone is in a different stage in their journey. A lot of self-care needs to take place on a deeper level. But you can be involved no matter your stage in development because you're always working on yourself... capable of having breakthroughs in the midst of your activism.

—Nahko, Nahko And Medicine For The People

As a greater number of individuals continue to pursue the path of healing, we are witnessing a time in humanity where people are discovering unique, and authentic ways to show up for others. Folks who have been consumed by substances are finding ways to connect with others and guide them along their path: that is the power of healing. When we find a way to grow from the very behaviors and tendencies which once insisted our decay, there is both opportunity and responsibility to help others discover the same. I am not saying that something is your authentic path or calling because you found a way to let go of it, but I am saying it could be. No matter your story, your journey and healing have likely been supported by others. The unfortunate reality is that not everyone has access to similar support. Each of us has the opportunity to serve as the cartographer (map maker) which guides others to realize their full potential. Again, this isn't to say your gifts insist you help others develop their own, but you might enjoy and find great purpose in it.

(map making)

We will grow together if we look to one another, when we believe it is best for us to crawl in a hole and die. Time, like your heart, will keep ticking so do not fear being defeated, we all are. A soul is measured in the moments after absorbing a crushing blow, and the moments after that. You are stronger than you give yourself credit for. You are closer to your dreams than you can conceive, and every ounce of you deserves to be happy. Embrace yourself, your potential, and your ability to be the inspiration you look for in the world.

(closer)

The permission that each of us seeks to belong, is within ourselves. We are fooled into thinking that acknowledgement from others is what grants it, and while it certainly helps, the sense of purpose through belonging which you seek can only be granted by yourself. When you recognize, embrace, and take responsibility of your gift by making it fucking rain, and never looking back. No one can do what you can do, in the way that you can do it. Remember that every time someone doubts you; remember that every time that someone is you.

(rainmaker)

Keep the faith, stay the course, let go, and let in. Who, and what are you letting go of? Who, and what are you called to let in? Without taking a critical inventory of your time and relationships, you likely already know which are reciprocal, positive, and worth holding onto. Reciprocity is a balanced exchange of time, attention, and love. Would someone understand the Christmas Spirit if they only received gifts but never gave them? Are you a good friend if you require help, attention, and time but never have it or offer it in return? We help because we're able, and we help because we care; but the care of another is rationally rooted in symbiosis (to the advantage of both). Our time here is limited, as is our energy and bandwidth to process, retain, and maintain information and relationships. Too often, relationships which require the most work (energy) offer the least in return. It reminds me of a song from one of my favorite writers, John Craigie: "I say, out of seven billion people, let the ones who don't love you go."

(limited bandwidth)

Loving yourself is to enter a divine cathedral, filled and decorated with the very ingredients which call you to shine. It is a pledge to show up for others, by always showing up for yourself, because a well without water, wills no wishes, nor quenches any thirst. It is a commitment to, and embrace of, treating each and every piece of you with love. It is an acute understanding of what you require to flourish, where you are lacking, and what you can live without. If everything was for everyone, nothing would be for anyone. Your song deserves the support of an orchestra, but only you can sing it; but before you can sing it, you must write it; and before you write it you must believe in it. We are asked (told) to believe in so many things, few of which offer us the return that loving yourself promises. The first and last sound we hear is likely our heartbeat, isn't it time we trust it? Isn't it time we listen to its wisdom? Isn't it time we will its wishes, and quench its thirst?

(divine cathedral)

Willingly wake with the rising sun to celebrate Sunday with ritual that soothes my soul. Deep breaths welcome the salty sea into my being on the edge of a breeze, lying between and beneath these palm trees. Coastal winds swirl with gusto, bringing storms to these waters for coming days, triggering memories of my love for storming-ocean-rains. Thunder and lightning crash as they cast darkness upon light, white caps sprawl the horizon beyond sight, their fury often lasts through the night. Don't worry about a thing, or what trouble these winds will bring, they come to soothe and sing good news. Blessings blow from sea to shore, love from my beating heart to yours. Let my love open the door, into seeing there's more here than meets the eye: so please take a deep breath and give faith a try. Faith in humanity that is one another; faith in Mother Nature and a vision where we coexist without such division due to ego, evil, and emissions. It is time to stop wishing and embrace vision, trusting the strings our hearts are tuned to, direction our souls called in, and our purpose in the place of hate; replacing despair with care for community, unity, and a common prayer to stare into the eyes of those who dare stand in the way, of a better world.

(stringed instruments)

Leaders must offer their people a helping hand, before community is practiced in any land. Strength comes from offering it to another. It must be given to be received: no different than love. The ordinary become extraordinary by sharing and showering others with their gifts. This process provides an opportunity, or catalyst for another to look inside of themselves for something they can share with others. When we are moved by another, by a cause, or by a set of actions that trigger an emotional response, I believe it serves as a portal between universes. We are conditioned to suppress and mask our emotional spectrum, even though it is what makes us human. Struggle translates into passion. Through our struggle, we learn the power of emotion: Its ability to motivate, or paralyze every action. Although it comes without expectation, or premeditation, a positive emotional breakthrough can be triggered by the most circumstantial experience. For this reason, never underestimate the power and the influence a random act of kindness can have on another's life, health, and happiness.

(random act of kindness)

You could have taught anyone, and anything, how did you choose special education?

My first teaching gig was at 19, up in DC in Anacostia, Southeast D.C. a non-profit. I was fairly naive, a little white boy, but the way we grew up in Immokalee (Florida), my dad was a Pasteur teacher, my mom was a nurse. It was ingrained that life has to be purposeful, and it seems purposefulness is set by helping people. People that have less. We have a lot, ethnically, culturally, compared to others we have a lot."

—Konrad Wert, Possessed By Paul James

Each challenge or circumstance we encounter is an opportunity to be better: similar to the way talent presents an opportunity to excel, or retreat. Which is the person you see in the mirror? Never forget, that it's a choice, not a circumstance. Circumstances reveal moments where choices are made, they do not determine what choices we make. While you may not be in control of your universe, you are very much in control of the choices that shape its potential. Let go of your fear, doubt, and ego, and embrace the beauty of unity through accepted dependence and love of others. Let your greatness shine through the weakness of another, as its light helps heal and harness their ability to make choices influenced by the power of belief, over the crippling weight of doubt. Do the right thing for the right reasons, and miracles may come to life. *Not all miracles appear spectacular.* The miracles we need are subtle: only noticeable at a glance; without the bells and whistles; beneath the roar of the crowd; delivered for those who can only manage a murmur. Circumstance quiets the sound of a voice, but we will grow with the choice to try and better listen.

(without bells and whistles)

From my bed I can gaze into the wild, wilderness, and world, but only I can choose to experience it. While much is learned from observation, there comes a time when we must step into the fog, embrace the rain, and find our way through to experience that which we've only imagined. Imagination is a magnificent and powerful tool, but with its gifts comes the burden of fear, falling, and failing; but like the lessons the wind bestows when sailing, these experiences reveal to us that falling is simply an opportunity to get back up, and failing only occurs when we give up. Living lends lessons, space, and time to recognize and take inventory of blessings. What would we know of abundance, without scarcity? Perception steers us towards having, or lacking, but it is the journey between these dualities which reveals the contents of our soul; a reason for being; a reason for seeing; a reason for believing that the blessing of the lesson will far outweigh our fear of its dismay.

For this reason it is better to wander than wonder, to fall than fright, to hurt than want, because only experience can reveal how much of your fear is an illusion; and how many of your limits are self-imposed. Your capability ensures your culpability, the very way your journey ensures your growth. Safety does not connote success, nor does it offer thrill. Love and life are in the living, making space for abundance to be given; but it is no matter of wishing, waiting, or hoping—seek out your purpose in the wide open—under the moon, under the stars, aside rivers and streams, where people are. People like you who make mistakes, curse, break bones, get lost, get scared, fall down, get up, learn lessons, and build a better life in a better world with each blessing.

(step into the fog)

No matter your potential it is imperative to learn to slow down, find calm and cadence in your breath, and ensure your life is fulfilled if you hope to continue filling others. Those who use their creative gifts and expression to heal hurting hearts and minds, often learn this lesson the hardest. Helping others can feel like an addiction we learn to endure despite its detriment to ourselves. It is easier to neglect personal needs when consumed by the intoxication of inspiring and empowering others. Whether you make music, write, dance, cook, paint, or otherwise create, each medium demands an intense energy transfer if it has any hope of being spectacular enough to touch lives. Purging emotion is draining, however, energy deposited into the world through artistic expression is readily reciprocated with great enthusiasm.

(energy transfer)

Until we are happy with ourselves, it is difficult to inspire happiness in others. Misery loves company, because being miserable is selfish. Joy emits from the belief in the reason we are all given life: to love, and help one another; to remind one another of our potential, beauty, and responsibility to honor our inner guide. While serving others we discover that we are healing parts within ourselves that may have been long-aching. We are social creatures that desire acceptance and validation from those we admire: from those we liken ourselves to. By surrounding ourselves with positive influences, we challenge ourselves to be better; to help others rise, and discourage our vulnerability to be consumed by fear. *The bloodline of a community runs through its ability to comfort, encourage, and provide a platform for one another's gifts to surface.* Community is collaboration over competition: collective good over coerced, individual advancement.

(collective good)

There are few problems in this world for which we are not the origin; which on a positive note means we are capable of discovering solutions once we open our eyes, and accept our role in all things beautiful and devastating. We are not helpless. Exhale. The life experience is intimidating when we allow ourselves to be overwhelmed by the faulty infrastructure present in all things. Meditation enables the individual to focus on something so simple as breath, to counteract the darkness of doubt with the illumination of learning and growth. Growth occurs when and where we least expect it, and that is precisely when, where, and why we need it most. Great satisfaction is derived from a roadblock navigated, storm weathered, and panic transformed to ease. Our emotional grid often holds the cipher to even the most exhausting enigmas, so we must care for our bodies, trust our hearts, and slow our minds.

(cipher)

Hone your sensitivity. We have been conditioned into believing emotions are a weakness, but they are one of our greatest strengths, when managed. It is the ability to feel that enables us to endure when it seems we cannot. It is a blessing to perceive the feelings and emotional condition of others. Our sensitivity is a well from which we harvest vision, insight, and a guiding light to illuminate the road before us when darkness lingers. Guide by feeling. *Cherish the moments you are brought to tears for a feeling you can't quite explain.* Those who make themselves vulnerable by wearing their heart on a sleeve, grow mindful of others happiness and cathedral of emotions.

(harvest insight)

Often, we isolate ourselves and those who love us by trying to bear the weight of the world on our own. Troubled times find us all. Some more than others. Some unlike we can or will ever know. It sucks when someone you know and love is suffering such a burden, yet you haven't the slightest idea. I believe we all have an image of ourselves that we wish to protect, an image that is at risk when we open up and share our deepest fears. Even if it is with the people we love. There are too many good things in this life to let pain and darkness overtake us. We must find what is ours in this life and no one else's. I am not talking about an occupation, or a hobby, or even a lover. There must be something inside each and everyone one of us that is worth holding on for. I'm not saying it's easy to find, but I am saying it's necessary. Have faith that you can, and you already have begun to.

(begin to)

Each of us holds the keys to the kingdom. That which could benefit us most, typically hides in plainest sight. As a result, we learn to walk by faith. Our vision is distracted and distorted by trivial variables. My personal evolution was leveraged upon my willingness to trust my intuition and imagination, which both I credit for the progress in my spiritual journey thus far. These lives we live are not one way streets with a beginning, middle, and end. They are four-lane-freeways with an infinite number of moments, begging us to remove our head from the clouds, listen, and engage those we rub shoulders with, whisper words to, and heal with our loving embrace. It will take a miracle for man to embrace his true potential by recognizing it in others, but for the sake of this story, I believe in miracles.

I believe in them, because I am one. Just like you. Our existence is contrary to the universe that surrounds us. We spend so much time and energy questioning our origin and purpose, while in reality, our purpose is our origin. We are here to help one another grow. Life insists on life. Our purpose resides in our willingness to protect all living things. There is a distinct difference between protection and possession. Living, breathing organisms are not to be owned, controlled, or dictated to. We protect because we are able. We protect because it is in our design. We protect because vulnerability is a strength that lesser beings prey on.

(miracles)

It does not count as helping someone when you hang your help over their head. Helping doesn't require receiving. Helping comes from the need, and ability to do so. The need which we've experienced ourselves, and have been blessed with a helping hand. The ability born within us to recognize wants from needs, and a person deserving of kindness. A person who could use a break: a person that hasn't got one in a while. A person who helps others even as their ship is sinking. A person who bleeds so his or her people don't have to. A person filled with light that is being encroached by the shadows, because experience is heavy. A person down, but not out. A person who inspires hope by breathing. A person who endures pain, so others hurt less. A person who suffers, so others suffer less. A person that achieves flight in the face of gravity; creation in the face of destruction; peace in the place of peril; balance in the midst of the perfect storm. If you choose to help, remember what it is you're choosing. You are choosing goodness. Idealism in a flood of realism; romanticism, trapped in a jungle of carnivores; optimism, while gasping for air in what may be your final breath.

(jungle)

I imagine heaven to be a place where everyone was greeted with a smiling face. Where precious moments on hatred we did not waste. Where love filled the oceans and streams. Where kindness showered a kingdom like the sun showers trees. Where no man or woman was made to beg on their knees. Where peace, love and happiness were a law like gravity. Where kindness overflowed like lava from a volcano. Where there was no exceptions to just who chose to be exceptional. Where honesty was a strength and not a weakness. Where God was food on every man, woman, and child's plate. Where faith was a helping hand to whomever required one. Where song was sung in nonexclusive exultation. Where dance was the obvious solution, and not the distraction. Where love and passion were the only guides.

(heaven on earth)

I fell in love with my human species, and it's proving unconditional. Despite tragedies, crime, greed, and egocentricity—I love mankind. I am moved by our ability to triumph over pain; to hang onto hope when there appears to be none; to inspire light in loom of darkness; to be broken but not defeated; to live in honor of those who sacrificed for the blessing; to help because we feel our duty to our brethren deep in our bones; to smile because we deserve happiness; and to love because it is our purpose and most pervasive form of experience.

(unconditional)

To be the best, you must first internalize that you are not. Growth is more prevalent in those who recognize its need. It is this causal relationship that renders talent both a blessing and a curse. For some, talent is the reason to work hard, and develop their gifts. While for others, it is a crutch which handicaps the necessary growth that only comes from hard work. A gift given is too often taken for granted. It is this logic which has taught me to recognize great strength, where perceived weakness, or disability is present. Each of us is given an opportunity to ask ourselves the question that others spend lifetimes avoiding: "Do I play the victim, or the hero?"

(question)

Open yourself to receive the very love you so readily give. You've been asked to carry this great weight as a testament of your deep seeded character, generosity, and commitment to others. The Hero's Journey calls you because it's where you have always belonged. Your sacrifice and struggle do not go unnoticed, nor will they define or confine you from the great heights you are meant to soar. Today's blessings are yours: do with them what you will; share them with whom you wish. Source is gazing into your eyes, hands moving from thighs to hips, please embrace the day's shine, and don't be too gloomy to embrace a kiss on the lips.

(allow)

We are wild, we are fierce, we are free thinking, free feeling, emotional creatures with both chaos and peace rushing through our veins. We are unpredictable, we are dependable, we are aloof, careless, careful, and often with an excuse. We are the antithesis of the riddle you seek to solve, undo, see through, and unglue, if only for some seemingly absolute, yet relative truth. We are imperfect, yet empowered despite our immense scrutiny and scour; counting the hours spent reducing ourselves to our greatest flaws; never living up to measurements, yet making ground navigating stars. We are brilliant and basic; epic and tragic; hopeful, hopeless, magic. We are a sentence that doesn't end. We are a story reaching completion because we've forgotten the endurance required to turn the page. We are wisdom, and its absence. We are alive, but are we well? We are human, but it isn't endless. We are dying, but it isn't the end of us.

(we are)

When confronted with oppression, and a heavy ruling hand intended to control, confine, and condemn, each of us has the choice as to how we shall either react, or proceed. Overtime, these next steps become the foundation and philosophy upon which our lives are built, and lived. Whether it be troubled waters, or smooth sailing, my life is given greater gumption, clarity, and hopefulness within the capacity, and effort to help lift others. When you are feeling lost, lonesome, angry, muted, or invisible, look around, everyone needs your help: especially those who don't know how to ask.

(next steps)

Each of us has been on a unique, difficult, and potentially beautiful journey over the course of the pandemic years. I hope that most of us have a more acute understanding of what we're fighting for, who we are serving, and why. I have observed a world intent on igniting fire, just so it could tune in to watch it burn like it was but another Netflix binge. I have an unhealthy relationship with that world and don't offer it much of my time or attention. I believe we oughta be having conversations about the things we love, admire, and are able to absorb hope, positive energy, and a sufficient reason to carry on from. It is time to live, love, and let go.

(attention)

CHAPTER 5

CULMINATION

Deep within our skin and bones resides the pervading need to be moved in a collective direction, driven by unity and purpose as we take a step towards one another, and all inhabitants of this planet. While we have constructed a world divided and defined by unnatural walls to keep us from experiencing our natural selves, the separation between us simply serves as a reminder of how much we need one another, and the environment which provides our ability to be - at all.

In a world that wages war with words and weapons it doesn't quite understand the pervading effect of, music offers hope in the form of genuine expression, vulnerability, and truth. Moved by rhythms, soothed by melodies, music shines light upon the revelry of words, the spontaneity of dance, and the possibility of healing through harmony.

Last night The Parliament Room at Otus Supply was gently caressed and blessed by the soothing sound, sight, soul, and "Grace of a Woman".

Mother to this earth, mother to this life, mother to the creative force which pulsates through my veins. Elephant Revival served as a satellite to the full moon, beaming its most exhilarating and climatic energy to cleanse the emotional burdens buried beneath our skin. Despite our unalienable differences, each and every one of us is a unique expression of the same beautiful thing — and the sooner we let go of our pain and suffering — we will recognize ourselves in all living things.

Are you hopeful that the harmony in music can help heal the hurt in the world?

I am hopeful. I am hopeful. Because, there's a lot of work we have to do together as a species and the way we are in relation to this planet. And it's not the kind of work we can try and tell each other how to try and be as human beings, or chastise or reprimand each other into conforming to some kind of harmony with this thing that we're a part of. I think what will bring us there if we're able to do it — is a sense that music brings and art brings that we are inextricably a part of this beautiful thing — and we are all expressions of the same thing. So, we're affecting ourselves when we affect anything else that's in it. It's what we are.

—Bonnie Paine, Elephant Revival

You are beautiful. Just in case no one has told you lately, we all need you. Even though I don't know your name, or what you look like, I believe that we are one. Born with a heavy heart and shining smile, longing to dance among the stars we gaze to. Drawn to those who recognize that love is a beacon of light for those lost in the darkness. Moved by he and she who live to lift others, even when they are weak. Inspired by our ability to leave fingerprints on the lives we are blessed enough to be a part of. Hopeful that together we can heal hurting hearts and minds, offering our time, energy, and care to ensure others are reminded that they are seen, heard, and loved. Optimistic, that goodness will prevail and offer its opposition no shelter from the storm. Your divine purpose is calling, can you feel it?

Made in United States
Orlando, FL
27 May 2023

33558024R00088